seasons *of a* girl

poems by
brooke
davidson

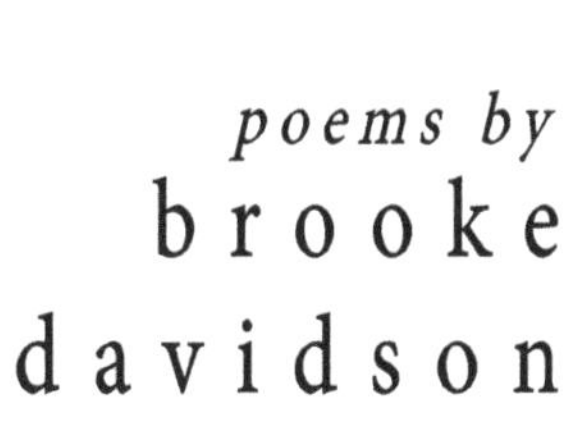

Seasons of a Girl

Cover Art by Autumn Toennis-Tsirigotis
Layout & Illustrations by Jenay Valencia

First Edition: 2021

Printed by Kindle Direct Publishing in the U.S.A
https://kdp.amazon.com/en_US

For Dr. Sexson, who helped me to more
consciously dance for the sake of dancing.

And for Crosby, who helped me see that
creating this book was a part of that dance.

Table of Contents

the birth of a poem (a preface)

the poem and the soul
are inextricable --
a tangled nest
of a thought from the supermarket, and an image
from the drive to work last tuesday
and the color of the worn persian rug in the cafe corner.
what seems, afterwards, the product
of a well-kept mind
was only a half-seen image, appearing suddenly
from the fog beyond the windshield:
1 word
and then another clicking by in the obscured headlights,
my pen racing
to keep up
for if a single one is missed so quickly will it be
reabsorbed into the mist.
the poem
is no formulaic creation; no pre-planned rhythm or script -
it follows only the beat
of my heart
of the neighbor's 90's r&b
of the bellowing cows across the way --

the pulsing of this in-duplicatable moment alone.
it contains no mulled over topic or line,
but rather the texture of that wooden floor
and the feel of that summer-in-winter rain -- warm to the touch.
and it is only after pouring (pulling? prying?) the words onto the page
that the picture clears. only after
can even i say what it "means"
(as though its creation and existence were not meaning enough).
sift through this nest;
tug and twine and tangle
and it will only break to pieces.
but maybe,
it will break open.

summer.

{the season of vitality}

i will taste wine on my lips
and hear wind rushing through the willow
out my kitchen window.
my bedside table will house books
whose pages are worn thin
from years of calloused fingers working their way through;
tracing those familiar lines.

my body will ache knowingly,
singing of its years of use --
scars like roadmaps of all the places it has been.
and my hair will hang in a long braid,
its course gray strands woven together
like the many stories those strands do carry.

that furrow of my brow -
evidence of contemplation -
will have etched itself permanently into the canvas
of my face.
alongside it, the evidence, too,
of laughter
and awe
and so many days beneath the sun.

i will leave this earth alone,
but with a heart full of memories -
each year richer than the last.
for as my body decays and falls apart,
what's inside will have only more cracks
through which to shine.
more cracks through which to shine.

she sits outside on a hammock chair
writing and sipping wine -
her feet bare in the warm summer breeze.
a storm brews overhead,
thunder rumbling its way to a roar
and the wind chime becomes suddenly serious about its job.
cows call louder and in greater frequency,
already headed to the trees at the bottom of the field.
and the first fat drops fall -- one splashing the ink on her page.
in response, she closes the worn leather cover
and fastens the brass latch.
“klaus! come on boy!” she calls,
half-ducking, half-dancing,
full-laughing
through the rain.
the dog jogs over and the duo enters the house
where she hurriedly opens all the windows.
the thunder now in her bones,
she breathes in deep
and listens to the symphony
of rain on a metal roof.

these summer storms bring life to more than just the flora

pale gray skies
and the scent of wet earth
greet me
as i drive down darkened roads.
the river has risen and rushes brown
next to the highway.
beyond it
suddenly green fields kiss
terracotta cliffs that disappear
into low hanging clouds.
i flip through a few songs
searching for a fit
until i find it
in the silence
between two waves of frequency.
radio off and windows down,
i drive this road
simply
because it is here.

“but isn’t ease… lazy?” he asked her.
“not at all,” she replied,
“ease is simple. quiet. subtle. soft...
but lazy? oh no.
we’ve trained our whole lives
for busy.
we brag about long hours worked
and short hours slept.
we relish in the flurry of a long to do list.
but to say ‘no’
or to choose silence --
to simplify or to surrender --
these things we have not been prepared for.
they may lead to ease, yes,
but they are not e a s y things at all.”

she has a voice like nostalgia -
like spontaneous road trips
across state lines -
and when she sings
i become unstuck
in time;
a vortex
of memory
and thought
and dream
blended into this
one
single
breath.
everything becomes beautiful,
and nothing hurts.

last two lines are inspired by *Slaughterhouse V* by Kurt Vonnegut

hers is a tale of trees.
first came the willow on her grandparents' farm -
the curtains of leaves
that denoted entrance into the fairytale world,
each perch a different place in make believe.
next came the cherry sapling.
the sweat and tears and hours of hiking
the surrounding terrain
colored this one special.
for even in those years of teenage annoyance,
she could recognize the value this place held.
after that came the lightning-struck cottonwood --
the first tree in a home of her own.
it was a shade in summer
and a topic of conversation every windy Wyoming night;
it was where the kitten yowled that late October afternoon,
waiting to be found,
and where her eyes naturally fell when surveying
the beautiful land that was hers
as she wondered:
who else has loved this tree before?

the older
I get,
the more I realize
how few memories
come from days with to do lists,
and how many
come from having fun
for the sake
of having fun.

.

as for me,
I want to remember
the days
I spend on this earth.

the heatwave finally broke
and a cool air whispered
into each open window.
i laid in bed:
my face exposed,
cold,
refreshed.
my senses awakened
as though from hibernation.

a desert evening in mid-July

sometimes
i become so saturated
with this life
that joy
d r i p s
from my skin.
i glisten
with wonder.
i revel
in the unfolding.

slow moving water
and chattering birds:
these are the sounds of contentment.
and those sounds do i hear frequently.
but a soulful, story-song and leather soles
stepping and sliding
across the floor --
these are the sounds of life.

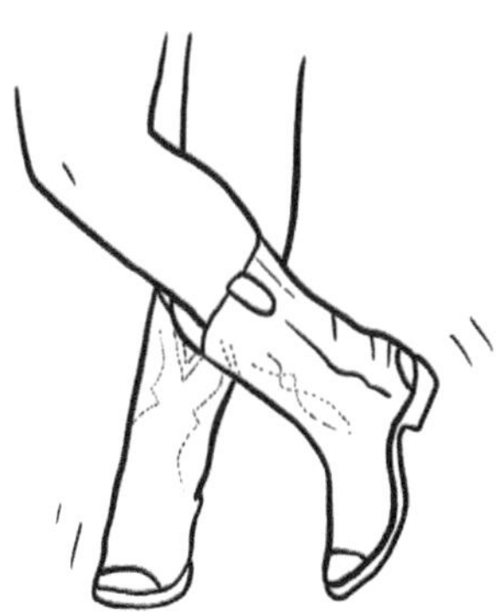

some days
it is enough to sit on the back porch and watch the dog
chase squirrels.
some days, however, i need more.
i need to be filled to the point of bursting
with life so present and true that only movement --
abstract gesticulations played out in time
with my heart
which, in turn, beats in time
with the music --
only that can fully express what it means
to be here
on this earth
in this very moment.
some days
i need to be so connected with this body,
so aware and in-sync with it,
that i am all together apart from it;
all together a part of every other atom in the room --
pulsing as one.
for in that moment i realize that i am not,
nor ever have been,
the water droplet
but only the water itself.

tidy up the house,
turn off the phone,
sweat or cry it out.
like the yellowing grasses of summer
need those darkened, stormy clouds,
we, too, need fresh winds
and our own cleansing rains.

the question
often arises:
do you want to
fit in?
or
do you want to
b e l o n g?
(i've always been one for sincerity, myself).

nothing in the natural world
blooms
and flowers
and bears fruit
year round.
and here you are,
so ignorantly expecting it of yourself.

realistic expectations

wind rushes through the tall grasses
like some half-remembered song
and i can't help but wonder
where those atoms have been
besides here.

awakening

there are moments
to root deeply
and stand the storm.
and then there are moments
to spread your arms
and let the wind
sweep you away.
you must be flexible
and willing
to do either.

when i look back
onto that year of new beginnings
i often wonder
just how i made it through.
but
novelty
and excitement --
adrenaline
and intrigue --
often blunt the edges.
it is only when those feelings fade
that the challenge
truly begins.

autumn.

{the season of change}

there are no strangers
under the warming autumn sun.
here
we sit in swaying grasses,
feeling every minute
the air grow colder.
night descends -
stars
and winds
and winter
in tow.
"it will snow tonight," you whisper,
"i feel it in my bones."

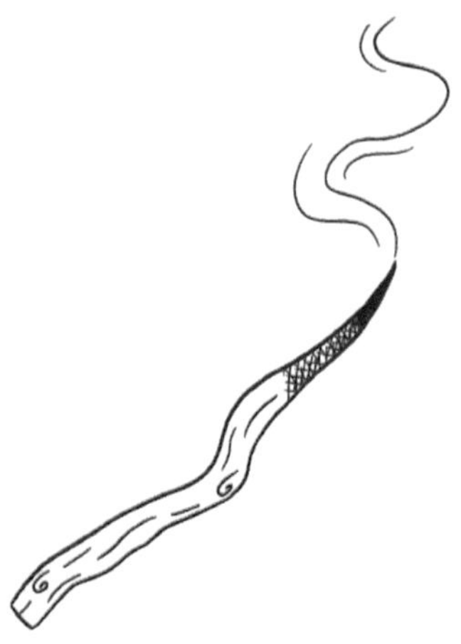

the first time the word left his mouth
i told him that i liked it,
and he used it like a branch to stoke my fire.
but now
the end has turned to a smoldering coal
and as he extends it back to me like false peace offering
the scent of burning flesh fills the air.

"darling"

silly human
observes the tree grow
and blossom.
and when the cold fall winds come it is she
who falls --
into sorrow and longing.
silly human
thought herself outside of nature;
thought herself an observer;
thought herself good at change.
silly human,
swept away in grief, doesn't realize
there is beauty
in this moment
yet.

there's no hindering what's natural

"the problem," he says,
looking down at me from atop the young horse,
"is that i tame them too much.
i just take the fight right out of them."
and i laughed,
making some comment about how that couldn't possibly
be a bad
thing.
but i don't laugh now
as i look into the mirror thinking
that is what has happened to me.

the breaking of a girl

tuesday. the morning is foggy on the farm,
a sure sign of winter's approach,
and the chill clutches at my bones through my skin.
i, like the season, hang in some sort of in between.
i am the first snow, melted by noontime;
the leaf dropped in an evening wind;
the moon, a vague cloud-covered glow.
i am weary-eyed and restless all the same.

humans have seasons, too

what propels
you?
what pushes
you to try
explore
create
something new?
what works its way into your very
b o n e s
and thus animates
your every movement?
(and who would you be
without
this?)

we are all just searching

you call me
thursday morning,
  emptiness in your hands,
and you ask if anything will ever be normal again.

i wake earlier than necessary
the following day
  and drive to work for want of anything else to do.
smoke-laden skies lend to the softest of sunrises,
  and just at the point where the sunrise
    and moonset
  appear equal within the skyscape,
i cross the north fork bridge
to see 2 elk on the gravel bar below.

the river holds the (rippled) moon's reflection
  and the elk's coats
  appear red-tinged from the sun,
and i am struck
  by the strangeness
of this eerie and beautiful oasis
amidst the low, flat, dry desert
which surrounds.

indeed, the image will haunt me for days to come
  as i wonder,
will anything ever be normal again?

blue sky highway, early morning commute

baby iguanas
spend their first day of life
outrunning racer snakes.
and here we are:
bickering over whose turn it is to make dinner.

perspective

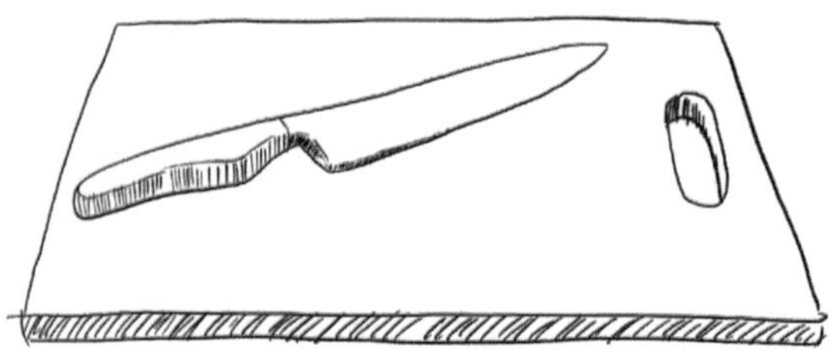

i worry for the young girl in the grocery store
trying on a shirt she doesn’t like
because it is “in style”.
our days are too few
for itchy tags
and seams too tight
in the armpit.
style
has always ranked second
to sincerity
anyhow.

i look in the mirror to see lines
in my face.
the movies tell me
i ought to be worried.
advertisements promise
creams to smooth it all away.
but life experience causes me
to sigh in relief.
“fewer gazes will follow me now” i say to myself --
and i feel safer already.

the reality of being female

how quickly these days pass - one folding into the other -
until suddenly the morning greets you
cold
and dark
and lush.
the trees release their leaves as a tangible reminder that we,
as part of nature,
must also shed what is dead.
must also pool our life within.
must also die to bloom yet again.

autumnal frequencies

“thou shalt not steal”
does not just mean merchandise at a store.
it is also when you discard dirty clothes to the floor
and thereby take another’s time
as they pause
to pick them up.

we steal (unthinkingly) daily

it is hard to love.
to stay in the game
to remain active and engaged.
an abundance of distractions
judgements
and comparisons
crouch eagerly at our fingertips,
awaiting a chance to jump through.
and yet,
our choices are our own.

fairy tales help no one

when words fail
and the light begins to dwindle,
let yourself stop searching.
choose instead
to sit. and breathe. and be.
to feel the autumn sun on your skin -
here for now, but waning.

there is beauty in this fading

the problem
with slowing time
is that you want to remain
sped up
within it.
the only way to slow things
is for you yourself to slow,
also

the western paradox

winter.

{the season of reflection}

i held you in my dreams last night. then woke
to a heart cracked open.
i fall asleep to dreams come true
but am mourning you
by morning.
this is me.
missing you.

the aching of your absence

three pictures.
that is all that connects then
and now.
three measly moments wherein i thought to grab the camera.
and even as i depressed the shutter to a blurry half-image
i thought "this could be it. i will keep this.
just
in
case."
what i didn't realize (even with as mindful as i attempted to be then)
  was that pictures really don't help.
sure, there is a certain softness to them,
  but so closely followed by pain and remorse and (unjustified) guilt
  that it seems not worth it.
we look back to see rose-colored scenes, their edges rubbed smooth,
  and we forget all the working-over it took to get there.
we forget that for weeks and months and years
  we turned that jagged stone in our hands

  only to tear and bloody
   our palms.
we forget how heartbroken
 and surprised
  and disoriented
we were, despite
all the mindful “preparedness,”
we look towards the future and alternate
between feeling absurdly
 hopeful
and irrevocably
 sorrowful
because in spite of all the time that has passed
and all that we have done to heal
(can’t you see these calluses on my hands?)
we
do not
forget.

on grieving

just because you are placed into
a box
does not mean
that you must stay there.

feel
for the edges,
the seams,
the worn out corners.
explore
in every direction
until you push enough
to let the light seep in.

and then,
push harder.

there are so many footprints i have left:
melted, grown over, covered in windblown dust
--
long forgotten by the land itself. and yet
still those steps live on within me.

the places that shape us

somedays
i step into the bathtub,
the lake,
the river --
coating myself in water
just so that these tears
won't feel so stark
upon my skin.

i guard my little joy fiercely.
i've seen how quickly it can dissipate;
i've seen how fully it can inspire.

here (for now)

the delicious half-light of a winter's morning
provides soft contrast between the rigid fence-lines
enclosing fields of pillowed snow
and the hazy, gray-blue mountains behind.
i watch
as each parcel of land
        cluster of trees
        herd of horses
clicks by --
each a life and a story
  i will never (really) know.
warm lights within distant(ish)
  windows,
cause me to question
  the history of this place
                this person.
but as each mile ticks by on the old car's odometer
the places whisper away -
just another thought lost
to time
and space.
another visceral interaction on the surface of this earth
                      this life.
something altogether
        disconnected
      despite being woven into the very same tapestry
            as myself.
every. single. day.
we pass through in this manner:
untouching and untouched
by the surrounding (enveloping)
worldscape.

on interconnectedness & happenstance

i once lived in the desert
where white winters were much forgotten
and poorly understood.
for white equated to snow angels, snowmen,
surely a school-wide snow day.
but here,
white only means black
ice
and high-stakes drives
to low-reward jobs
wherein we look out the window and wish for sweatpants
and a hot, lightly-spiked drink
and a couch to cozy up on.
they say the snow is whiter on the other side of the mountain
and this has surely proven true.
but still,
there is something irreplaceable in either scenario:
the silence
and softness
that folds itself into each open space
until everything is insulated
from the cold - by the cold -

and only a soft crunching can be heard.
i once lived in the desert,
where white winters were much forgotten,
but not this year
where for 6 days no schools opened, for no buses could run
because what city invests in a snow removal budget
for a 3-month winter forecasted
to have 9 inches (total)?
and while this pre-christmas snow falls heavy, it brings
the deep, in-my-bones aching for dry heat and red dust
and the tightness of skin
slightly burnt,
and coated in salt.

a pre-christmas snow

i wake with poetry
on my lips,
but by nightfall taste only
salt tears.

i look over the wintery river
and wonder how it is that two people
can occupy the same space
yet remain so very separate.

i feel like the clouds that hang up in the mountains:
restless
yet stuck swirling in place.
something
has got to give.

maybe we are simply too good
at being alone.
maybe our independence
has become our burden.
maybe, like slabs of ice within the river,
we've drifted too far apart
to come back together.

but eventually,
ice melts.
two rigid chunks
d i s s o l v e
into indiscernible droplets --
into a single unified current.

this isolation
may just be
temporary.

i want to believe
that i can be happier;
that i can be more useful to this world;
that this is an
o p p o r t u n i t y
to explore
and not a
p r o b l e m
to address.
i want to believe
that there is
m o r e
than this
out there,
and that i'll stumble into moments of raw
m a g i c
if only i let myself
s t e p
off of the trail.
call me ignorant.
naive.
hopeless dreamer.
but these fairy tales in my bloodstream
ring truer
than the rat race
i've been running.
and baby,
i want
to believe.

today,
in the swirling winds of chaos,
i found beauty.
i let go
and danced
with the falling leaves --
i lifted my chin
and surrendered,
and as my grip loosened
my breath came with unprecedented
ease.
the lightness there,
but fleeting.

this life is but a practice

a rolling hum
pulses through the air
riding each wave of warmth,
and i sit deeper in my skin.
i watch the flames dance,
my body swaying in rhythm,
for it is a song i, too, carry.
and as the flames consume
each block of wood
i find yet another
connection --
for i, too, must digest
each experience.
i, too, must take in each moment
knowing
there is no such thing
as return.

like fire

when the morning light
oozes softly
through the fog
and the birds
are muffled to a whisper,
find yourself
a empty fence rail
and look across
that sacred stretch of land.

this is your home.

today i whispered gently to myself
“the dip of each wave is only so deep
because the crest is so very high.
just keep swimming.”

this, too, shall pass

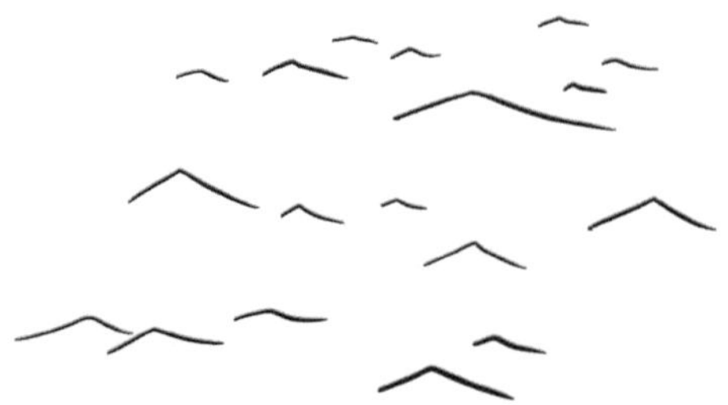

the moon
glowing
upon the icy-topped river.
this is the soft ferocity
with which i want
to love you.

these tender moments float me

strong woman
holding her chin high,
her weathered hands
open
at her sides.
she sees the hard edges
of this world
and meets them
with love
unending.
your clenched fists
are no match
for her wit.

be like the banks of the river:
let water course through you
and do not
g r a s p
when it goes.
maintain structure,
direction,
integrity,
but also know
that sometimes the water will come
r u s h i n g
in such volume
that you will find yourself altogether
c h a n g e d
upon its leaving.
learn to widen and narrow -
to change course of direction -
without utterly collapsing.
for this is how rivers
outlive us all.

spring.

{the season of renewal}

i have stopped
visiting the gravesite
of the person
i once was.
the flowers there
have dried up
and turned to dust,
like the bones beneath them.
with every exhale
comes deeper release.

it's okay to change

a storm brews on the horizon -
clouds boiling in anticipation,
their darkened bottoms like wombs
made round with what is yet to come.
i stand amidst hip-high grass,
the air warm and still around me,
and fix my gaze upon the tumult in the distance.
as the grasses begin to stir,
a shadow crosses and the clouds draw together overhead.
i lift my face
and the first cool droplet splashes onto my cheekbone.
the storm hasn't yet broken,
but it has arrived.
and i am here,
palms open,
ready to receive it.

driving home from work
i am met by rain so strong
it sounds like gravel
on my windshield.
flash flood warnings
pop up on my phone
and before the screen turns black
the sun has reemerged.
this, too, is how i cleansed myself of you --
suddenly,
in a passionate fury,
without lingering.

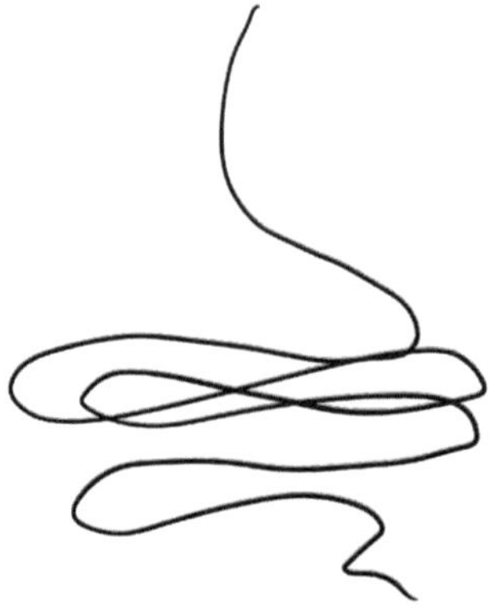

there is something in the undoing -
the unraveling
of what was so purposefully
woven together
of what once acted as a support
but now -
each strand loosened -
lies limp
beneath your feet.

an invitation
to begin (again)

not every page can be brilliant.
there must be scribbles
and rhythmless stanzas -
frustrations made visible in ink.
these reminders of your own humanity are, afterall,
the kindling
for the fire
yet to come.

the creative process

there are seasons
of comfort
and seasons of growth --
seasons of joy
and pain
and learning
(oh, the learning.)
there are seasons
of head held high
and seasons
of heart cracked open.
oh, darling,
there are seasons.

you belong
in places
where your kindness
elevates you
instead of
invites others
to push you down.

lean into the wind
and raise your chin
to the sun.
you are a child
of this world --
do not
tiptoe
in your own home.

walk like you belong here (you do.)

what if
instead of trying to
please.
impress.
compete.
and guess.
you instead chose
to be
open.
attentive.
okay with yourself as you are
right now.

i chose to water
only what was willing to grow.
and thus,
you slowly shriveled up
and turned to dust
at my feet.
i cannot say i am sorry.

she holds truth in her heart
and fire
in her eyes --
kindles it with mischief
gentle as a feather.

unstoppable

in the moments of in between -
the seconds of lightness
and ease -
i float, fly, fall
into myself.
where i've been waiting
with open arms
all along.

becoming

the thing about returning to your roots
is that in your absence
they continued to grow.
and now you run your fingers
along their gnarled, gritty surface
and learn them
as though for the first time.

hometown visit

remember darling --
there is so much more
to this life
than being loved.
you are here
to be love
itself.

on being that for which we wish

do not let others' ideas of you
compete
with your idea of you.
it is okay to feel
strength, beauty, power.
they will judge you either way.

unapologetic

a jagged, white scar
on the knuckle of my left thumb
reminds me of the summer i spent cutting fallen trees
from backcountry trails.
and on my knee resides a quarter-sized shape of africa
as a memento
of those winter weeks spent beachside.
i trace these markings like a map
and always
they guide me back.

the maps we always carry

some days creation rolls within my stomach.
it stretches its limbs and crawls up my throat,
crouching
on my tongue,
and at the slightest parting
of my lips
bursts forth.
you cannot hold your art captive.
give it an opportunity,
and it will find a way into this world.

what are we
if not chasing dreams?
if our purpose
in life
was to settle
it would be much easier
to do.

how we know to keep dreaming

people will undervalue
what they don't understand.
you must value it enough
for everyone.

our art is for us before anyone else

you cannot know
the wars she has waged
or through what she has persevered.
you assume
her smile comes with ease
simply because she wears it like a crown.
as well she should --
battled for,
and won.

the story of a girl

may you be strong and soft.
open and relentless.
passionate and content.
and may you be yourself
all the while.

on striking a balance

I hope
the to do list
that pops into your mind
upon waking
includes
sitting with your tea
in the cool morning air
and learning from the deer
who lie bedded
beyond the garden,
sinking into the stillness
while it's still there.

the end.

{and now, onto a new beginning}

just like a garden
left unweeded
will not produce
as abundant a bounty,
ourselves left unchecked
will squander
our energy
to that which
does not help
us flourish.

continue to prune away
anything
that pulls you
away from yourself.
you are the garden (and the gardener)

About the Author

Brooke Davidson is a writer, high school
English teacher, and yoga instructor as well
as host of a mindful living podcast:
The Practice (w/ Brooke Davidson).

Her short stories and poems have been featured in
a variety of publications over the past 5 years.
Seasons of a Girl is her first book.

Davidson lives in Cody, Wyoming with
her husband, Crosby, and their dog, Klaus.

https://brookedavidsonyoga.wixsite.com/seasonsofagirl
@brooke_being

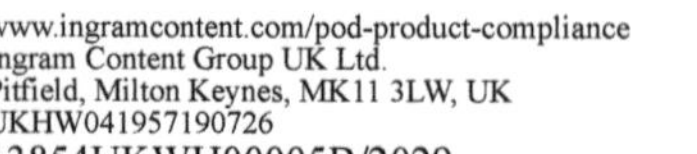
www.ingramcontent.com/pod-product-compliance
Ingram Content Group UK Ltd.
Pitfield, Milton Keynes, MK11 3LW, UK
UKHW041957190726
13854UKWH00005B/2029

9 798538 002825